The Things I Notice Now

THE THINGS I NOTICE NOW

Dennis Maloney

MADHAT PRESS
ASHEVILLE, NORTH CAROLINA

MadHat Press
MadHat Incorporated
PO Box 8364, Asheville, NC 28814

Acknowledgments:
Many of these poems have appeared, some in different forms, in the following magazines: *Pilgrimage Magazine, Earth's Daughters, The Path, LEVURE LITTERAIRE, Korean Quarterly, Kyoto Journal, The New Camaldoli Hermitage Newsletter, The Buffalo News, Queen of Cups, New Madrid, Pirene's Fountain, Fulcrum,* and *Plume Magazine;* and in the following anthologies: *A Celebration of Western New York Poets, An Outriders Anthology, Right Here, Right Now: The Buffalo Anthology,* and *Collateral Damage.*
    "Just Enough" was published as a chapbook by Palisade Press, Taos, NM, 2009; and a number of these poems were previously published in *Empty Cup,* a bilingual German/English edition published by Verlag Hans Schiler, Berlin/Tubingen, Germany, 2017.

Many thanks to all the editors and publishers who have supported my work over the years.

Cover art: Melissa Lofton, "Unnamed Ridge, Sunset." Copyright © 2017 by Melissa Lofton. www.mlofton.com

Author photograph: Elaine LaMattina

Library of Congress Number: 2018956251

ISBN 978-1-941196-77-9

www.madhat-press.com

First Printing

—

Other Books by Dennis Maloney

Poetry

Wanderings
Rimrock
I Learn Only To Be Contented
Return
The Pine Hut Poems
Sitting In Circles
The Map Is Not The Territory
Just Enough
Listening to Tao Yuan Ming
Empty Cup
The Faces of Guan Yin
Windows

Translations

Naked Music – Juan Ramón Jiménez
Dusk Lingers: Haiku of Issa
Windows That Open Inward: Images of Chile – Pablo Neruda
The Landscape of Soria – Antonio Machado
The Stones of Chile – Pablo Neruda
Light and Shadows – Juan Ramón Jiménez (with others)
The House in the Sand – Pablo Neruda (with Clark Zlotchew)
Between the Floating Mist – Ryōkan (with Hide Oshiro)
Seaquake/Maremoto – Pablo Neruda
The Naked Woman – Juan Ramón Jiménez
Isla Negra – Pablo Neruda
The Landscape of Castile – Antonio Machado (with Mary Berg)
Unending Night: Japanese Love Poems (with Hide Oshiro)
The Turning Year: Japanese Seasonal Poems (with Hide Oshiro)
I Pass Through This World – Ryōkan
The Poet and the Sea – Juan Ramón Jiménez (with Mary Berg)
Hyakunin Isshu: 100 Poems by 100 Poets (with Hide Oshiro)
Tangled Hair: Tanka of Yosano Akiko (with Hide Oshiro)
Three Material Songs – Pablo Neruda (with Mary Berg)

For Elaine, together on this journey

Table of Contents

4 – Life Among the Ruins

5 – Border Crossings

1

Just Enough

Why do I desire to see things
as they are without me,
or claim as my ancestor
the mountain hermit in a cave
with no distractions, no companion minds?
I don't know. Who wants to know?
                    —Chase Twichell

Empty-handed I entered the world
barefoot I leave it.
My coming and going—
two simple happenings
that got entangled.
                    —Kozan Ichikyo

1

How hard it is
to take
what is given
and say yes,
just enough

2

The pond mirrors
space and stars.
The moon paints
it gold. Mind,
here is your peace.

3

The sea glitters blue
open to sky and solitude,
shifting mysterious depths.
We too have stars
and blue depths.

4

Above broom-swept ground
tight new maple buds
unfold delicate leaves
enjoyed with no thought
of autumn.

5

Don't give me the whole truth,
but sea for thirst, sky for light.
Give me a glint,
as birds bear water drops
from bathing.

6

Lost in daydreams.
In a far field a butterfly
swirls around spring grass.
I am a child again
sailing with clouds.

7

Fingers of mist
caress the mountain
softly touching the treetops.
Suddenly the palm closes
—mountain gone.

8

Warblers haven't
begun to sing,
but I hear spring
in the cascade's roar
pouring over the rocks.

9

Is spring fragrant
in dreams or reality?
I fall asleep
near a mountain
far from home.

10

The reverberations
of the temple bell
keep on coming
out of the bush clover
as memories echo.

11

Evening near the river,
willows cascade along the bank,
a scene for a painter.
Throwing on his raincoat,
the fisherman heads home.

12

Some days the pond
has utter clarity
—a distant mirror.
Other days
it is clouded by rain.

13

Beads of morning dew
cling to bamboo leaves,
glittering like pearls.
Morning sun just piercing
the veil of clouds.

14

Deep in the forest
the city drops away.
A bird song greets the morning
and is answered.
Sweat pouring down my face.

15

On the mountain trails
of the self
—hot summer sweat
step after step uphill
no destination in sight.

16

Two friends eating lunch
when the floor begins
to shake beneath them.
Both look up to notice
that no one else seems to notice.

17

Another cup of sake
with old friends
and new acquaintances
now friends
forever.

18

The bamboo,
its heart empty,
has become my friend.
Water with its pure heart
has become my teacher.

19

Shops named Beauty & Lucky.
As if they could bring
what is promised
in that attraction
of blinking lights.

20

Twenty-five years ago
I first saw Kanō's
swirling dragon.
Today, I am still learning
how to ride him.

21

No coming
no going
here together
sharing tea
—what a beautiful bowl!

22

Sen-no-rikyū said
tea ceremony is simple.
Heat the water,
make the tea, drink.
How did they complicate it so?

23

Tips of cedar
sway in the wind
as we pass by
tethered to a cable suspended
between sky & earth.

24

White egret, great blue heron
stand in the Kamo River,
the sun setting.
Dusk settles over the river
suddenly evening.

25

At Shisho-in
the mountain's heartbeat,
the pulse of the pine,
evening's faint bell
—all one.

26

A young woman
performs endless prostrations
to the Shinto mountain spirit
accompanied by chanting & gong.
Her mother hovering above her.

27

Buddha, what was your word?
Wisdom, compassion,
loving-kindness?
All your words are contained
in your name: wake up!

28

The teacher taught without words
finger pointing quietly upward.
It praised, punished, pierced the heart,
until a student trembled
and woke up.

29

You didn't ask to be born
but here you are living
in the everyday world.
There is so much,
one life is not enough.

30

A good poem
should smell of tea,
earth or newly split wood.
A few words woven together
to make a home.

31

In the old days
the teacher said
find a need and fill it.
What is that need?
Only the road will tell you.

32

The horn played
by a Buddhist monk
echoes up the hillside.
A yamabushi chanting
under the mountain waterfall.

33

Evening dew shimmers
on the strands
of a spider's web.
How long I wonder
will it last?

34

One robe, one bowl,
one poem drawn
from this wind-blown life
heart bright
as the full moon.

35

On Mt. Kurama I walk
paths you once walked
and remember the passionate
intensity of your love songs,
sleeves wet with memory.

36

A traveler at midlife
climbing a dark path
through the forest.
City noise fades
to a solitary bird song.

37

Mist dissolves everything
living and dead,
each universe reflecting another,
reflecting itself from every other
in this jeweled net.

38

Years spent in
meditation halls
wandering from teacher to teacher
polishing, polishing the mirror
—now break it!

39

Some days I would gladly
shave my head and
take up the monk's robes,
but I am too fond
of this world.

40

The temple bell silent
until a swinging log
beats deep iron,
a voice reverberating
in and out of the pines.

41

If you're kin to the pine
you'll live long,
glisten in the rain,
be lively in autumn,
beautiful in snow.

42

The river deep in my mind
is singing again.
A windless calm reaches me
from the cool night,
but where are my words?

43

I open the window to see
the living dark before dawn.
Orion roams the sky,
forever on the hunt.
The plum tree, bare and black.

44

Dawn birds twitter,
breaking the traveler's sleep.
A crescent moon lingers;
I'm alone
at the sky's edge.

45

I hike mountains and
fathom quiet mysteries
of thought, different
trails that merge
into forest and clouds.

46

Chrysanthemums slow
to bloom. I find
no joy in autumn.
The heartless west wind
blowing my gray hair.

47

Last fall we walked
along the Kamo River
as the leaves turned.
This spring a friend writes
to tell me you are gone.

48

A homeless beggar
lives under the bridge
like Kūkai in days past,
and he writes his poems
on the walls like Han-shan.

49

I do best alone at night
with the secrets my lamp
sets free from
a day that asks so much,
bent over a task never finished.

50

At the fox shrine
supplicants leave messages
asking for luck in love and fortune
—a chorus of cicadas joins
the conversation between old friends.

51

The journey home
a thousand miles.
But in my dreams
I have been home
three times before dawn.

52

Cicadas have exhausted
their voices
on the hillside.
Once again
temple bell startles.

53

The ten thousand things
of this world,
pass them on
—ours to use
but not to own.

54

When autumn comes
even ancient
mountains
take on
a deeper hue.

55

I grow lonely
watching the moon
flood fields and hills.
If only I had a house
outside autumn.

56

An old man needs no visitors,
just a few friends
and what family that remains.
Give his door a wide berth,
as if no one lived there.

57

Scoop up water and
the moon is in your hands.
Brush the flowers
and their fragrance
lingers on your sleeve.

58

On the rock-strewn path
wind rustling leaves
of bamboo grass.
The only other sound
your own footsteps.

59

Mountain stream
just the thing
to quiet the mind,
climbing the narrow trail
before autumn.

60

When a man reaches old age
he has no need of men
and their noisy world.
What he needs is peace
and time to face what is next.

61

Listening to
pine branches snap
under heavy snow
—all night long
cold mountain hut.

62

Cold wind clears
leaves from the trees
night by night
baring the garden
to moonlight.

63

The window iced over
when I woke.
But I was warmed
by a good dream
and embers in the hearth.

64

A bundle of contradictions
this life
part bodhisattva
part hungry ghost
but fully human.

2

The Things I Notice Now

Rained again last night.
Street slowly drying.
Sunlight's not too bright.
I don't believe it's trying.
I never used to care.
It wouldn't cross my mind.
You'd be surprised,
The things I notice now.
—Tom Paxton

A WILDERNESS

We wandered
my friends and I
in the summer field
that was our wilderness.
Suddenly we were far from the city
in a lush green forest
of grass taller than our heads.
Full of rough places
and low spots where we held mock battles
of cowboys and Indians
pirates and space demons.

Or caught up
in the buzzing of life
alive in that field
we captured crickets
in our cupped hands
and watched as a spider
sucked the life
from a fly
caught in his web.

One summer our territory
this fragile forest
was mowed and leveled
with backhoe and dozer.
Square holes were ripped
out of the earth and walls raised
to form houses
with trim lawns
surrounding them.

What we thought
was vast space
a wilderness
was nothing more
than three or four houses
at the intersection
of two streets.

Buffalo Diner

Streets slick with rain.

I step back in time
—a vintage '50s diner.
The lone black busboy
limps along behind a cart,
cleaning the tables.

I nurse a cup of tea,
waiting for the last bus.
Desperation is almost
palpable in the air.

The waitress dreams of Elvis,
sings along to Karen Carpenter
on the jukebox:
"Rainy days & Mondays
always get me down...."

I go back out into
the hot humid night.

Sometimes in Winter

1

I move inward
with the first snow
falling on the city,
gathering
like dust
in the dark places

2

Day and night
snow falls
without pause,
creating a
stalled magnificence

Walking outside,
the storm plays
a harsh music,
leaving its icy score
frozen on my beard

I trudge toward home
like a German soldier
headed for the Russian front

3

There is silence
in falling snow,
ice forming on
a slow-moving stream,
a clean whiteness
filling old tracks,
nestling in the forks
of an old cottonwood,
filling grassy fields
until only the heads
are above suffocation

4

The enormous wind
howls over the lake
and up the frozen streets,
hurling walls of white
past the office window

People are thrown against buildings;
the nativity scene shudders
as the four walls explode
and dance down Main Street

Abandoned cars strewn about,
drifts high as houses,
for five days the city
is almost still

as people learn
to walk again

That same wind,
less intense later,
carves the snow
with delicate feminine curves
soft as a sculpture
by Jean Arp

5

Everything empties
into white

LETTER FROM THE OLD SOD

Sandymont
Miltown Malbay
County Clare
December 12, 1932

My Dear Brother

It is now drawing near Christmas
and time to write a few lines
to those that are far away
hoping to find ye all
in the best of health
as this leaves everybody
here at present thank God.

Though I don't write often
father and Martin and wife are fine,
also John and wife and family
but we don't see James
but very seldom.

Times are a bit hard nowadays
in every country as well as here.
The laborers are the best off
here now for they have work
in the roads and quarries
and get five pounds a day.
There is nothing for cattle,
we couldn't even sell
one beast the fair day.

Mr. Connell he left us in a way
that we won't have a bite for anything.
I didn't need put anyone out
looking for him he landed here
August 16th just the same as a bailiff.
He is married and wanted to buy cattle.

Then the first of November
she was to be here.
But a week later he disappears
leaving the cow to Tim Hogan
to milk and take home with him.

So he lands one night around ten
having wife and luggage without
one spark of fire nor light,
nor one to say God save you
or where did you come from.

She seems to be a nice woman alright.
I met her in church one morning
but I didn't go near them or invite them.

He used to tell some she was from Galway
another time from Mayo and now she's
from East Clare. She is Mrs. O'Connell
anyway but nobody knows her name.
He'd come and go just like the
Caseys and the Carthys but I've
said enough about him for now.

Michael Hogan is home for the past few months.
His father was buried a month before he came.
I have no more to say just now.
Father has landed with his walking stick.
Wishing ye all a very merry Christmas.

Your fond sister

PORTRAIT

after Antonio Machado

My childhood is memories
of a small neighborhood
in the south of Buffalo
learning to sing Irish lullabies
and drinking songs.

My youth, twelve years spent in
the schools of the Vatican
memorizing answers to
catechism questions I could
not believe in. I walked
away, out into the world
and learned the ways
of the natives of this place,
discovering what fragments remained.

As a young man I discovered
the world of poetry;
my mentors taught me
to hear my own song,
discover the beauty
of contemporary expression
and the ancient trail of poetry
leading back two millennia.
Not to follow in their footsteps
but to seek what they sought.

I shun the shallow ballads,
the political double-speak of the day,
and those clever verses without meaning.

I try to separate the real from
the pale echoes and among the voices
listen only to the one I converse with
always my sole companion.

In the end I owe you nothing
but the lines I have written.
I have sustained myself
working to provide
the roof over my head,
the clothes on my back,
the food and bed
that comfort me.

In a small garden in Kyoto
there is a boat-shaped rock
that will take us to
the other shore.
When that day comes
I will sail away leaving
no footprints or wake.

The End of Innocence

Gathering a book of fairytales
for my new granddaughter,
I found a glossy political flyer
stuck inside from a long-
forgotten campaign.

Robert Kennedy for Senator
from New York and vague
memories of meeting him
in an American Legion hall
with an awkward handshake.
I was all of thirteen.

There were the complaints
of him being a carpetbagger,
since we all knew he was
really from Massachusetts,
but he was a Kennedy after all.

This was not long after
the end of the age of Camelot
and those rumors of Marilyn.
1964 and my own coming of age;
the Beatles arrived in New York
and appeared on the Ed Sullivan show.

I was learning a new geography
from Da Nang to Montgomery,
Selma to the Ho Chi Minh trail.
I learned of trees that bore
strange fruit as I figured out
how to navigate this world.

In a few short years we went from
Meet the Beatles to *Sgt. Pepper.*
By 1968 he declared his run
for the presidency and was
assassinated a few short months later.

On the turntable we hear
Mick Jagger growling......

> *I shouted out*
> *Who killed the Kennedys*
> *when after all*
> *it was you and me..........*

The Summer I Learned What Work Was

for Phil Levine

The summer I learned what work was,
I was fourteen, the same age
as my eldest granddaughter,
working for sixty cents an hour
farm wage, when the regular
minimum was more than twice that.

I wanted a new bicycle and rode
my old one with the bad brakes
early each morning to a truck farm
at the ragged edge of the city, where
houses petered out into small farms.

The crop rows seemed endless,
thinning lettuce seedlings, weeding
then bunching radishes, beets,
crawling along on my knees,
feeling the pain in my back
under a hot summer sun.

These days we drive through the
Salinas Valley; plumes from irrigation
sprays dance over faint green lines.
Crops laid out in strict rows far as the eye
can see to the hills on the horizon,
Mexican migrants bent over in the hot sun
picking the crops that will feed the nation,
but we call that work by a different name.

JANIS

Who was that boy
of seventeen wandering
the streets of New York City
alone for the first time,
hip to the music
but not the street,
still living in the house
of his father between
the vagaries and scars of youth.

Fifty years later warm waves
of memory flood the brain
when I hear your voice again,
preserved now on this
scratchy acetate disk,
remembering that humid night
of early August '68:
at the Fillmore East, you
take the stage with Big Brother
wild hair, granny glasses,
bangles, bracelets, baubles,
vibrant, electric, prancing,
breasts almost bouncing
out of a tight dress,
hiding the wound that
would never heal.

Voice bursting out, caressing
each word with tenderness,
each song ravaged, shredded,
singing down the wind
like a raging gale.

The audience awed that
one human being could
give so much of herself away.

LETTER TO JAMES WRIGHT

Our fathers labored
in the same bitter factory;
they just called that hell
by a different name.
Yours in Hazel-Atlas Glass and
mine in the lampblack and chemicals
of Hewitt Robbins.
They endured week after week
that turned to decades,
learning to tolerate
what no man could ever
learn to love.
A life that wears a man down
to a poorly functioning machine.
I worked two summers
in that factory
and tasted the bitterness.

We both ran
from that ugliness,
frightened we
would be trapped
in a life there too.

I now work
in that place
where you labored,
facing the white page
to conjure a world
beyond the one into
which we were born.

SUMMER OF LOVE

The department-store signs
declares it is the summer
of love in 2009,
and the displays
are full of peace signs,
jewelry, granny beads,
peasant blouses, headbands,
and scarves.

How far from
the summer of '67 and
the Haight with
Janis Joplin, Jefferson Airplane,
the Dead and Quicksilver.
The Diggers providing
food, clothes and spirit.
A few months when,
in our innocence,
we thought love
and goodwill
would change everything.

At home I filled
my mother's old pans
with Rit dye
and soaked the folded
and rubber-banded T-shirt
into colors creating
tie-dye patterns
of infinite design
as I tried to decipher
my own young world.

REFLECTIONS IN THE REAR-VIEW MIRROR

An age when young men
prowled the highways
in souped-up jalopies
with a slant-6 or V-8
and gas was thirty-five cents.

When I was a kid
we didn't have a car
but I remember
those '50s commercials
on the black-and-white TV
—*You can trust your car*
to the man who
wears the star,
the attendant in the
crisp uniform and cap
The ad claimed they
would put a tiger
in your tank.

Now every time we
absent-mindedly fill up,
we fill our tank
with the oil leaking
into the creeks and
swamps of the
Niger Delta, can you
feel the noose tighten
around the neck
of Ken Saro-Wiwa?

Our cars that run so efficiently,
the oil platform
engulfed in flames,
choking estuaries
from Louisiana to Alaska.
Objects in the mirror are
closer than they appear.

3

Searching for the Sky

LETTER TO SANDY TAYLOR

They tell me you are gone,
yet I keep seeing you;
they tell me that when you met
Lady Death you gave her
a big kiss on the lips,
with a little tongue,
and embraced her
with a huge smile,
a twinkle in your eye.

Even now I think I spy
the corona of your cigarette
and you sitting
at a sidewalk café
in Copenhagen, Guadalajara,
or some unknown capital,
sipping a cup of coffee
among the grand architecture
and ruins of another time.

I sit on the ocean shore.
Seabirds bring your message,
wrapped in waves and kelp.

BREATHLESS

Hearing Creeley read
at Harvard circa '72
words flow
slow, deliberate,
with nervous energy,
significant hand gestures
sweeping air

Leaping from
chair to blackboard
uni-verse   re-vers-ible
one-turn   re-turn
all in a breath
and of breath

A sequence of numbers
for Robert Indiana
square / circle / triangle / star

Puffing a glowing cigarette
you pause between stanzas
to light one
from the other

And so on years
later in Buffalo
sharing poetry, beer
and conviviality

On the bye and bye
there are more
words to be said

but the labored breath
of a body
that wants to keep
on breathing
leaves you breathless

Unnatural Acts

The sleek grey dolphin
endlessly circles and circles
the confines of the tank,
glides through the water
with longing memories
of the open sea, turning
in graceful loops
of pure energy.
But trained to perform
unnatural acts,
he leaps from the water
to kiss the startled child.

PROTECTIVE CUSTODY

The dusky seaside sparrow:
a few ounces
of floating spirit,
black and white feathers.

Its range of a few miles
of cord grass
and tidal marsh,
battered first with
DDT and then
an engineered flood,
Its habitat slipping away.

A half dozen,
all males, were kept
in protective custody:
a $60,000 cage
at Disney's Magic Kingdom
until the last one
slipped from this world.

CHILDREN'S DRAWINGS

The drawings are rough and crude,
like those my son
or your daughter
brought home from school,
full of awkward lines
and smudged colors.

Blue, green, red, yellow ...
but unlike those drawings
of houses with oversized doors and windows,
with colorful rainbows & stick figures,
a bright yellow sun dominating the sky,
with children at play
in tree forts four stories high,
these are different.

These are drawings
of children caught in war.
Images of planes
and helicopters dropping bombs
on huts which burst
into orange-red flames
and soldiers in green
with machine guns and machetes
to kill the fleeing peasants.
Written in shaky captions,
*Shut up you guerilla wives, we sharpen
our machetes for your heads.*

THE VINEYARD QUEEN

Sunlight creates shimmering patterns
on the bay of crystal.
The midsummer wind coming cool
off the water tousles my hair.
On deck two children roll about
in the rhythm of boat on waves,
cry for help and imagine drowning.

Scavenger gulls glide by
vainly searching dense patches of sea.
Buoys signal sandbars, shallow water;
fishermen struggle to haul half-filled nets
over the side, into the hold.
Passing the docks, longshoremen load cargo
in the hold of a Tokyo steamer.
The downtown Boston skyline creeps forward
until it looms large overhead.

The rhythm of waves beckons,
calling me to come deeper ...
underneath and flowing
toward the center of things
on filaments of light.

What Gets Left Behind

for Patti Smith

Amelia Earhart's bones
and spirit still wandering the
shoals of the Pacific

Marilyn's smile
and sultry voice singing
"Happy Birthday
Mr. President"

Virginia Woolf's bed
and a room of one's own
strangely silent,
a pocket full of
River Ouse rocks

Mapplethrope's slippers,
Robert Graves's hat,
William Blake's death
mask & imagination

Rimbaud's fork and spoon,
Roberto Bolaño's chair,
Herman Hesse's typewriter,
Hendrix's burning guitar
at Monterey all seared
now in memory

WINE TASTING

A light refreshing taste
with aromas of green apple,
lemon grass and melon.
Vibrant flavors
of pineapple, peach, and pear.
Palate-pleasing flavors
that lead to a crisp finish.

Strawberry, spice, and floral
hints greet the nose
with just a touch
of pepper and oak.
Deep rich hues
of plum and blackberry
merge with broad tannins
and pleasant astringency.

Scents of sweet berry
entice the senses
with wisps of cola,
licorice, spice, and notes
of cassia and vanilla.

A vibrant aroma of dark berries,
with a touch of spice and subtle
smokiness, a deep garnet, a touch of spice,
rich bramble fruits and faint licorice
on the nose with wisps of pepper
and citrus peel this zin
is ready to party.

We raise a glass
to the clever prose
of the copywriter
who has made so
much from a simple grape.

AFTER THE FIRE

for our neighbors
who lost their homes in the Sobranes fire

1

A few sparks from
an illegal campfire
ignite a hot summer

and years of drought
that explode into
a raging inferno.

A wall of fire overwhelms
and devours fifty homes
in our canyon.

After the fire we stayed away
out of respect for the fire and
our neighbors who lost everything.

The artist, a lifetime of journals, studio,
finished and unfinished work,
the musician, guitars, mandolins,

decades of musical notations,
others, the usual household contents,
artwork and moments of a life.

Joni Mitchell sang *cause I've seen some*
hot hot blazes come down to smoke and ash
speaking about a human relationship

but here the land is scoured by fire,
hills layered in ash, trees contorted
in shades of grey, black, almost white,

looking like a sudden snowfall
in mid-August. Now they sift
through the debris, what

remains of a life,
sparkling shards of glass,
glittering like jewels.

2

It was months later when I first
walked the scarred area with
a friend who lost almost everything.

The winter rains had washed
away the ash, and nature began
to heal as it always does,

grasses and wildflowers
returning, leaves on
the few surviving trees.

Tibetan monks spend weeks
meticulously constructing
a mandala from thousands

of colored sand grains
that will be dismantled,
sands swept into the sea.

The monks intoning
Impermanence, impermanence,
when you are empty, wait.

SEARCHING FOR THE SKY

for Elaine

Searching for the sky
an iridescent green hummingbird
that somehow found her way inside,
fluttered her wings,
hurling her slight body
against the skylight glass.

I fetched the extension ladder
and held it while you ascended,
cupping the bird gently
in your hand and descended
out into air and light.

She lay in your outstretched hand
perhaps stunned or frightened
before lifting off, astonished,
into the air in search of the sky.

Visiting Red Jacket's Grave

for Maurice Kenny

1

White men will come
asking for my body,
wishing to bury me.
Don't let them take me,
bury me among my people.
I have no wish to rise
among pale faces.

Red Jacket told his wife
just before his breath faded.
Yet even in death
they did not let you rest
but dug up and moved
your bones across town
to the white man's cemetery
far from the folks at home,
the place of the basswoods,
sacred grounds along Buffalo Creek.

In a small neighborhood park
a stone marker remembers
the reservation cemetery
a mile from where I was born.

2

I drove Maurice to Forest Lawn
Cemetery to visit Red Jacket's grave.
There the gravestones of the chiefs
sat in a row—Little Belly,
Young King, Tall Peter,
Deerfoot, Red Jacket,
Destroyer Town, Captain Pollard,
and General Ely S. Parker.

In the heart of each
an American flag was planted.
I kept the car engine running
while Maurice pulled out each flag,
lifting them easily from the earth
and snapped the stick neatly in half.
He said I was pretty brave for a white guy
as we pulled away slowly,
done causing trouble for that day.

3

Red Jacket's Seneca name was
Sagoyewatha, "Keeper Awake"
as he was such a great orator
no one fell asleep when he spoke.
When a missionary came to try
and convert the Seneca, Sagoyewatha
gave the following reply:

*Brother, our seats were once large
and yours small. Now we have scarcely
left a place to spread our blankets.*

*Brother, you say there is but one way
to worship and serve the great spirit.
If there is but one religion why do
you white people differ so much?
Why not all agree,
since you read the same book.*

*Brother, our religion has been
handed down by our fathers to us.
It teaches us to be thankful
for what we receive,
to love each other and be united.
We worship in that way.*

Brother, if you white people
murdered "your savior,"
make it up among yourselves.
If he had come among us,
we would have treated him better.

Kyoto in Spring Song

for Edith Shiffert 1916–2017

My first spring trip to Kyoto
in over forty years, and some
of the sukura cherry blossoms
have waited, cascading in displays
of single and double blossoms.
The last time I was here in spring,
streetcars rattled down
the avenues of the old capital.
Now they have been replaced
by silent trains running underground.

I rarely remember my dreams,
but several days before your death
you visited in a dream. It was
before sickness took your mind
and hobbled your body. I don't
quite remember what you said,
but it may have been,
Resting on the earth
who needs satori or faith?
Embrace what holds you!

Here I sit in my hotel room
across from the Imperial Palace
with eight boxes of your belongings
to sort after the clothes, cosmetics
and household items were given away.
Half of the books to a used-book store
the other half given to friends as keepsakes,

old bank books and years of tax returns trashed,
papers, notebooks, photographs sorted for the archive.

What's left of a life well lived?
Homesteading on the big island of Hawaii
during the '40s, scanning the coast
to spot Japanese submarines,
then Mt. Si to the Yukon
with your first husband who
suggested you type his failed novel
instead of doing your own writing.

You soon took leave and moved
on to Seattle to delve into Asian Studies
and poetry with Theodore Roethke.
Then in your mid-forties, you embarked
on a journey to Kyoto, a proper introduction
and a one-year teaching job in hand.
Over five decades spent
walking these mountains,
visiting temples and shrines,
becoming the hermit-poet you
wanted and chose to be.

A few nights later the journal
that takes its name from this city
celebrated thirty years of publication,
bowing to the many artists now passed.
Beside the Kamo River
we read your poems by lantern
and candlelight, releasing them
back into the realms of darkness.

4

Life Among the Ruins

PESSOA CAFÉ, AMSTERDAM

for Franz Hammerbacher & Beatrice Fassbender

Between the streets
of red lights
and Central Station,
down the alley
past a canal,
we find the
Pessoa Café.

Ah, the first minutes
in cafés of new cities!
We raise a glass to
all those voices
we carry within,
but there are real
conversations to be had.

All of us see
ghosts before us.
How many masks
do we wear, the
waitress, the cook,
patrons sitting at
the other tables?

Pessoa said, *I'm an ascetic*
in the religion of myself.
A cup of coffee, a cigarette,
and my dreams substitute
quite well for the
universe and its stars.

Off in a corner,
he starts to fidget,
orders another drink,
pulls some paper
from his pocket,
scribbles down verses
on the back of a handbill,
fragments, teetering
on the brink of illegibility.

TRANSLATING OLAV HAUGE

for Olav Grinde

For three days
we have parsed
words and their
meanings, sound,
and cadence,
to capture the flinty
Nordic language
of Hauge's poems.

Near evening clouds
of wild doves return
to the canyon,
hundreds of wings
beating as one,
soaring in arcs,
landing in the
redwood crowns.

In the poems' faint light
and long winter nights
we see that darkness
he carried within
return, an unwanted guest.
But he persisted
among his shadowy ghosts
even in that rocky soil.

A Conversation of Birds

As dusk settles
birds return
to the date palms
in the courtyard
of the kasbah
after a day largely silent
in the hot desert air.

Suddenly hundreds
of conversations begin.
The birds gossip
and sing to each other.
A faint scent of oleander
perfumes the garden,
and as darkness falls
the conversations dwindle.

In the still and utter darkness
the stars come closer
than ever before,
galaxies spiral toward us,
and we are traveling,
leaving no footprints behind.

SHEPHERD

Dawn. The sparse crowns
of the olive trees
come alive with color.
At the end of summer,
brown fields are barren
and full of dust.

A shepherd sits
on the hillside
tending two dozen sheep.
He has never traveled
farther than his legs
or a mule can carry him.

Not much happens here,
but he knows the land
and his flock better
than he knows himself.
For hours he sits in silence.
What thoughts fill his head?

LOBA

for Alfonsina Storni

Alfonsina, you ran like
a *loba* to the hills, leaving
behind this world
dominated by men.
Refusing to be
snowy white
like the dawn,
you dared look into
poetry's pure eyes

She-wolf of the seashore,
sailing without ships or ports,
watching great birds
pass without destination.
The sea unlocked
its strange perfume
and rose through
the channels
in your spine.

When the flowers of death
blossomed in your breast,
you choose to return
to the sea, embraced
by the waiting
arms of kelp.

Broken English

In the middle of the Cold War
and near the end of the Vietnam war,
a Japanese friend and I
stroll the Kanazawa harbor
and find a ship emblazoned
with a hammer and sickle
carrying tree trunks
from some taiga forest.

Is this our enemy?
The evil, warned
about since childhood,
we were told to crawl
under our desks to survive?

We meet a sailor
grabbing a smoke
and converse
in broken English
and find he is not so evil,
just a working stiff
hoping for a bit of shore leave
to buy his son a stereo and
smuggle it back home.

UNCOMFORTABLE

Across from the Japanese
Embassy in Seoul is
a sculpture of a comfort
woman seated on a bench,

designed to make the
Japanese uncomfortable about
continued mis-rememberings
of their own history.

A survivor sits down
next to the sculpture
bearing witness
so the Prime Minister
cannot avert his eyes
while expressing vague regrets
just short of denial.

SINGLE-JOURNEY TICKET

Each day I walk a couple
of blocks to the Shanghai subway
past the greengrocer
sorting and washing vegetables
in plastic bins on the narrow walk
and enter the labyrinth
of security and metal detectors
to purchase my single-journey ticket.

Shuttling under the city
in tubes of light
through dark tunnels
to the street markets
and bazaars of the Yuyuan gardens
or to stroll the promenade along
the Bund surrounded
by 19th-century European architecture.

Looking across the river at Pudong,
which morphed in twenty years
from boggy farm land to the future
of commerce and business,
high-soaring cranes
and the visions of modern
architecture gone wild.

Never knowing when our
single-journey ticket may
be subject to abrupt cancellation.

Against Forgetting

for Jian Feng

After dinner in Beijing,
he wrote only *Remember*
as a dedication in
his volume of Chinese translations
of Emily Dickinson, as if to say,

Don't forget I was
a soldier in Mao's army
who fell in love with English,
a most dangerous affair,
for which he was
denounced and imprisoned
in the chaos of the fifties.

Banished to the mountains
for a decade of hard peasant labor
during the Cultural Revolution—
when everyone went mad—
he lost track of his family.

After the arrest of the Gang of Four
he became editor of an English-
language literary journal, translated
an anthology of contemporary
American poetry found
on an obscure library shelf.
Once brutalized, he was finally
freed from his sentence for
the crime of translation.

Hiking the Great Wall

We hike the Great Wall,
a spring breeze
showering us with
apricot blossoms.

Thousands of miles
with watchtowers built
to control borders, keep
the enemy from the gate
but the Mongols arrived
anyway. Today's emperors
wear different costumes

but are frightened by
the barbarians within
and without.

They try to scrub
certain words
from the vocabulary
but those words remain
hidden like an
underground stream.

They try to build walls,
virtual and real but
can no longer keep
any of their foes at bay.

Life Among the Ruins

High above the throngs
of tourists, in the scorching
summer sun, a worker,
unnoticed by most,
returns day after day

to sit patiently cleaning
the flutes of a small
section of a Doric column
of the Parthenon, not unlike
the ancient relative

who carved them
when the gods
and goddesses
of the ancient myths
were more real.

Later we stroll the paths
of the Agora, walking with
the ghosts of Socrates and Plato.

The Secret Within the Seed

Across the Ponte Vecchio
on the other side of the Arno River
away from the crowd of visitors
hiking toward Piazzale Michelangelo

overlooking the city, I stop to rest
in a small park full of children
gathering pinecones from
the adjacent trees and placing them

in buckets. An olive-skinned
grandmother strikes the upper
branches with a pole, knocking
more cones to the ground.

I thought all this industry
was to gather the cones as keepsakes
or toys before watching the children
strip nuts from the cones

and discard the empty husks, later
to garnish a lovingly prepared dish.
The secret within the seed.

MICHELANGELO'S PRISONERS

The sign tells us they
are unfinished, unlike
the smooth curves
of the grieving Mary
and the lifeless, almost
sleeping body of her son,
or the magnificent young David.

But I think you deliberately
left them unfinished,
the muscles of prisoner Atlas
straining under the weight
of the load he carries,
struggling to emerge.

These tanned,
muscular, sweating bodies
of the workers you sketched
at the quarries of Carrara
who cut and hauled
the stone by hand
still wrestle
to break free.

2

Border Crossings

for Jose Oliver & Tzveta Sofronieva

I keep translating words
into other words
which are mine
Who do these words
belong to?
Writer, translator, poet,
or to the language itself
For lovers or users of words,
this is the difficulty—
what gets lost is not
what gets lost in translation
but more what gets lost
in language itself.
                    —Alastair Reid

I

We gather in the Black Forest to explore
the boundaries, borders of language.
A border that is always
wandering, sometimes east, west. We never
know exactly where, always vanishing, breaking,
maybe inside ourselves.

Listening intently, I try to follow the patterns,
cadence of speech alive in the air and strange to the ear.
In conversation and poetry, we struggle to find the right words,
through the jolts and swerves of syntax, complexities of exchange,
the extravagance of lost syllables.

Sometime language borders are permeable,
where breath itself is a conscious action
that travels across languages and joins us together.

2

I have spent my life building
bridges between the shores of language
and culture, always straddling emptiness,
danger, wave by wave, a map of the world.

I have crossed the Pont Neuf, the Ponte
Vecchio, as poets have between reason and madness.
The Bridge of Sighs, the Charles bridge, the humpback
canal bridges of Amsterdam, a long shaky bridge,
always teetering. In the evening I wander the streets
of the city along these frontiers of our uncertain freedom.

3

In the capitals and squares of Europe
people gather to support the Falun Gong, refugees
fleeing Syria, and victims of the genocide in Armenia.
Under the Brandenburg Gate they celebrate the
World Cup win. I hear the rare chant of *Hare krishna,*
an almost extinct species in America.

In the dark shadows the nights of broken glass
reemerge as the persecuted are confused
with the persecutors, and marches and rallies
against all that is foreign stream into the night.

4

A dictionary explodes, sending words
fleeing toward the borders,
chased by those without name
toward a great unknown destination.

Words are refugees smuggled in hidden
train compartments, walking obscure paths
through farm fields, forests, washing
up dead on shores, lost at sea, crawling
under fences and over walls built to keep them out.

Words are on a clandestine voyage seeking asylum
in an unknown language, their passports thick from
collecting centuries of official stamps. One can't
over-estimate the amount of accumulated baggage.

5

for Fouad El-Auwad

The Syrian poet entered Germany at sixteen
and now reads his poems in both
the sonorous Arabic and the harder
German cadence. Both beyond my understanding.

After the poems come audience questions,
not about the syntax of the poems
and their wild unpredictable lines,
but the fractured country he left decades ago.
A country shattered into shards
like a precious porcelain Chinese vase
that hit the floor, hard. They ask
how the mangled lives and broken
cities can be put back together.

What is the poet's answer?
A storm is gathering over the world,
there are no victories,
we must learn not to be afraid,
all of us must learn to speak a new language.

6

On dark nights when I have no words
of my own, translations calm me, let me
jump deep in letter by letter,
soaking up the dampness of the words.

I hear a whispered sigh like the sea
in the dark, as both poem and self
exist in a constant state of becoming.

What draws us as translator to seek
an equivalent music from one
tongue to another? Affinities, a vibrancy,
listening to meanings that reside, flowering,
beyond the thickness of dictionaries.

Nibbling at the edges of the poem, we give
contours to shadows. How do we translate
the silence that lives between the lines?

I am a nomad searching for a language
in which I am a word unbound,
wandering between the world
we inhabit and the world we create.

7

On the Charles Street Bridge, artists sketch
people passing and jewelers
sell their wares. A small
band sings the Delta blues of
Robert Johnson, meeting the devil
at the crossroads; the melancholy Rilke blues,
and that unending struggle between poetry and life;
the blues of Kafka, and snow falling in winter,
the Václav Havel blues that changed everything.

Sing of the fragile moments of life,
beauty, and dreams, and all the love-
in-vain, train-done-left-the-station blues.

8

In the *word laundry,* the new vocabulary
no longer describes but conceals the slow
corruption of language. The incendiary
explosion of voices dehumanizes with
hateful words, the onslaught of disinformation.
In the *word laundry,* military campaigns
are named after nature, like *strong
cliff.* No one is responsible
for the earthquake, the tsunami.

9

For a few moments at Christmas one
hundred years ago, a brief pause in five
months of unbelievable slaughter and carnage.

The German and British soldiers
in the middle of a Belgian field stopped
shooting at each another, left their muddy
trenches and met in the middle
to exchange food, cigarettes, and gifts.

German beer for British rum.
They barbecued a pig, sang carols, played soccer,
startled by a sudden outbreak of peace.
Two days later the full fury of machine
guns and shelling resumed.

10

Every year after plowing fields of potatoes
and sugar beets some unexploded ordnance
works its way to the surface, an iron harvest.

The earth has become its own
last witness, coughing up reminders,
shoes, shells, eyeglasses, bones, razors,
a perfectly-preserved gas mask.

Neither side made much headway
despite artillery barrages so fierce
and long they wiped villages, roads,
buildings, and forests from the map.

A half-million killed or wounded,
one ton of explosives for each square meter,
turning the landscape into a lifeless swamp
lingering, the war that is never over.

II

A small faded black-and-white photo
of my great-great-grandfather at ninety
sitting on a stone wall with his dog.
Sandymount, Milltown Malbay, where
the farm falls into the sea. My grandfather
and two brothers came to America—one
was lost in the war to end all wars.

My grandmother also emigrated to these
shores and refused to speak of Ireland again.
Now I find myself at the county seat
in Ennis's hall of records
to obtain the birth certificates of my
grandparents so I can reclaim
what they left behind.

12

for Jimmie Margaret Gilliam

It is a summer of sorrow. Friend
after friend has crossed that final
undefined border without guards or
checkpoints between this world
and what lies beyond.

The body is at war with itself.
Insurgents plant roadside bombs, rebel
armies attack systems without warning,
and the warp and weave unravel,
leaving a ragged edge behind.

The last words written, a worn satchel
of poems left behind, lines rattling around
the fading brain. We can not barricade
our hearts against sorrow any more than we can
deny the joy of their being.

These fragile objects we accept
at the passenger's own risk.

Notes on the Poems

Just Enough
These poems are written in the voice of a contemporary hermit-poet living in a small hermitage near Nanzen-ji in the Higashi-yama region of Kyoto, Japan. Inspired by the classic Japanese hermit-poets, a lineage that includes Saiygō, Bashō, and Ryōkan, the poems grapple with the tensions between engagement with and withdrawal from the world but do not escape the complications and struggles of modern existence.

Tanka (short song) is the contemporary name for the *waka,* the main traditional form of Japanese poetry, which has been written for over 1300 years. Both the tanka and the haiku have migrated to the United States and around the world. The tanka in English is still defining itself and lacks a conclusive formal definition. Because of their compression, nuance and understatement of language, they often ask the reader to complete the poem.

19 Shisho-in is a temple in Kyoto.

20 Kanō's Dragon – Japanese painter Kano Tanyu was well known for his paintings of dragons. His best-known is on the ceiling of Myōshinji temple.

22 Sen-no-rikyū was the founder of Japan's formal tea ceremony.

24 The Kamo River is the main river that flows through Kyoto.

32 Yamabushi are Japanese mountain hermits, ascetics, and holy men who seek spiritual, mystical, or supernatural powers.

35 Mount Kurama, located northwest of Kyoto, is the birthplace of the Reiki practice.

   The poem refers to poems written by Yosano Akiko.

48 Kūkai, also known as Kōbō-Daishi, is the founder of Shingon Buddhism. He lived for a time under a bridge in Kyoto.

   Han-shan was a Chinese hermit poet.

64 A bodhisattva is someone who vows to work for the enlightenment of all sentient beings.

Hungry ghosts, beings with narrow necks and bloated stomachs, are a metaphor for insatiable hunger.

"Reflections in the Rearview Mirror" – Ken Saro-Wiwa (1941–95) was a Nigerian writer and environmental activist. He was hanged by the Nigerian military government.

"Uncomfortable" – Comfort women were Korean women forced into prostitution for the benefit of Japanese soldiers during World War II.

DENNIS MALONEY is a poet and translator. A number of volumes of his own poetry have been published, including *The Map Is Not the Territory: Poems & Translations* and *Just Enough.* His book *Listening to Tao Yuan Ming* was published by Glass Lyre Press in 2015. A bilingual German/ English volume, *Empty Cup,* was published in Germany in 2017. In 2019 a chapbook, *Windows,* with translations in several languages, will appear in Germany from Hochroth Verlag and a book of poems, *The Faces of Guan Yin,* will be published by Folded Word Press. His works of translation include *The Stones of Chile* by Pablo Neruda, *The Landscape of Castile* by Antonio Machado, *Between the Floating Mist: Poems of Ryōkan,* and *The Poet and the Sea* by Juan Ramón Jiménez.

He is also the editor and publisher of the widely respected White Pine Press in Buffalo, New York, and divides his time between Buffalo and Big Sur, California.